Letts

Framework FOCUS

D0433263

YEAR
9

Grammar

Louis Fidge
Ray Barker

How to use this book

Letts Framework Focus: Grammar books have been designed to provide a versatile resource, capable of being used for a variety of teaching and learning situations and by a wide range of teachers – specialists and non-specialists alike. They:

- contain 30 units of work, sufficient for one school year
- are straightforward and easy to use
- provide discrete double-page spread format for quick reference
- have a clear teaching focus
- contain differentiated activities for each objective.

Letts Framework Focus: Grammar books can be used in a variety of ways:

- They easily provide work for the whole class, groups or individuals.
- Use them to introduce a key literacy topic – as a lesson 'starter'.
- The structure of the pages allows for teaching a particular literacy issue to the whole class.
- Units allow teachers to focus on a particular issue if this seems a problem for an individual or group.
- Planned progression allows teachers to consolidate, develop and extend literacy work over the year.
- Each unit provides work for follow-up homework assignments.

As a lesson starter

The Grammar Focus provides a clear explanation of each objective with examples for discussion or illustration. Appropriate activities may be chosen from the range of differentiated tasks for discussion, or to work through with the class.

Group and individual work

These books are ideal for group and individual work. Teaching on the same subject can be realistically matched appropriately to individual pupils' abilities, allowing pupils to work independently.

Homework

The design of the material in the books provides an ideal solution to meaningful homework assignments – differentiated appropriately for each pupil.

Contents Year 9 Grammar

Objectives ....>

- To review the clarity of meaning in sentences.
- To search for, identify and classify a range of prepositions.

Grammar Focus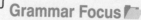

- A **preposition** normally tells you about the **position** of **something** or **somebody**.

  Prepositions tell you the **relationship** between one word and another, e.g. the relationship between two nouns:

  The cat sat <u>on</u> the mat <u>under</u> the table.

- **Compound prepositions** consist of **more than one word**, such as:

  apart from, because of, in front of

- Prepositions can also be followed by an 'ing' form:

  <u>By</u> working hard, he became successful.

- Some words may be used as both prepositions and adverbs:

  The farmer walked <u>round</u> his field. (preposition – because it is followed by a noun phrase)

  The farmer turned <u>round</u>. (adverb)

Starter >

1 Copy the sentences.
Underline the prepositions.

(a) The road goes across the heath.
(b) Ranjit walked through the puddle.
(c) When she was frightened she hid behind the door.
(d) The golden sun rose above the horizon.
(e) He leaned against his mother for support.
(f) The pen had fallen between the floorboards.
(g) My dad towed the car to the garage.
(h) Our dog ran suddenly into the road and the car swerved.

2 Look again at the sentences in (1). Explain which two words the preposition shows the relationship between.
For example:
The <u>water</u> poured down the <u>drain</u>.
'Down' links 'the water' and 'the drain'.

Practice >>

❸ Look at the words below.

| after, across, into, before, beneath, through, by |

Copy the sentences.
Choose a suitable preposition from the box to complete them.

ⓐ He was swept down the river _____ the fast-flowing current.
ⓑ The snake disappeared _____ the dark hole in the ground.
ⓒ I ran _____ the thief, but he escaped in a car.
ⓓ Grandma found the old letters _____ a pile of old books.
ⓔ I counted the money _____ taking it to the bank.
ⓕ When he pushed me, I fell _____ the window into the garden.
ⓖ Two enormous insects scuttled _____ the table in front of me.

Extension >>>

❹ Copy each sentence twice.
Use different prepositions to give each sentence two different meanings. The first one is done for you.

ⓐ The sergeant stood _____ his sentry box.
The sergeant stood in his sentry box.
The sergeant stood behind his sentry box.
ⓑ That motorway passes _____ the city.
ⓒ A strong wind was blowing _____ the west.
ⓓ My mum drove the jeep _____ the village.
ⓔ Felix the cat chased the mouse _____ the front room.
ⓕ The QEII sailed _____ San Francisco.
ⓖ In the film the cowboy jumped _____ his horse.

Feedback ↩

Words may be divided into groups, known as 'parts of speech' (or 'word classes'). Each part of speech has a particular job to do in a sentence.

The prefix 'pre' is Latin for 'in front of'. Prepositions are words that are 'positioned' 'in front of' nouns (or pronouns).

Objective ·····>

- To revise the use of apostrophes for possession and in contractions.

Grammar Focus

- **Apostrophes** may be used in **two** ways:

  – An apostrophe may be used in **contractions** (when words are shortened) to show that something has been missed out:

  do not can be written as *don't*.

  – An apostrophe may be used to show **possession** (that something belongs to somebody).

- When the owner is **singular**, we usually add an apostrophe and 's' after the noun:

  the house belonging to the girl = the girl's house.

- If the owner is **plural** and the noun ends in 's', to show ownership we put the apostrophe **after** the 's':

  the house belonging to the girls = the girls' house.

- When a plural noun **does not end** in 's', we show ownership by adding an apostrophe and an 's':

  the children's sweets.

Starter >

1 Write the contraction for these words.

(a) would not
(b) they are
(c) we have
(d) I am
(e) you are
(f) she is
(g) does not
(h) was not
(i) they will
(j) who is

Practice >>

2 Copy the sentences.
Circle the possessive apostrophes.
Underline the apostrophes that show letters are missing.

(a) We didn't clean the stain from Jack's overcoat.
(b) They've told us that we can play with Margaret's skipping rope.
(c) I'm always borrowing Hardy's novels from the library.
(d) My father's car wasn't ready at the garage.
(e) The women's rucksacks were left at my father-in-law's house.
(f) Greek myths are about heroes' deeds or lovers' troubles.
(g) I'll never look for eggs in those birds' nests again.

3 Rewrite the sentences above to show **what** belongs to **whom**.
For example:
The overcoat belongs to Jack. The troubles of lovers.

Extension >>>

4 Write sentences containing possessive apostrophes.
The first one is done for you

(a) a horse   hoof
   horse hoof = The horse's hoof had a stone in it.
(b) two lions   manes
(c) the bicycle   tyre
(d) my cat   fur
(e) the mountain   summit
(f) Fred the hamster   cage
(g) three cars   wheels
(h) the local farmer   fields

5 Copy the paragraph below. Place the apostrophes correctly.

   Lets look at this dinosaurs skeleton. Its made of hundreds of bones.
   I cant believe theyve all come from one animal. Its makers mustve dug
   up loads of animals in the countrys mountains. Collecting enough
   animal bones to make the skeleton realistic mustve taken many years
   excavating. Nobody knows what dinosaurs outsides looked like.

Feedback ↰

Using apostrophes correctly is important
to make your meaning clear. In this unit
you have reviewed the simple rules for
using apostrophes to show possession.

Objective ·····>

- To revise the variety of ways nouns make their plural.

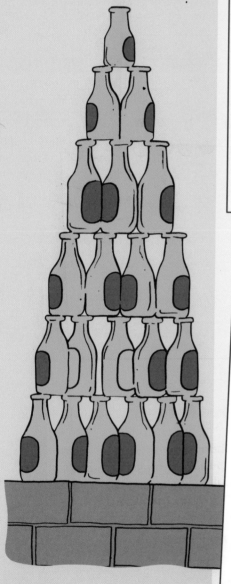

Grammar Focus 📁

- The most common way of forming the **plural** of a **noun** is to add an 's'.
  One green bottle or *twenty green bottles.*

- When you form the plural of most nouns ending in 'ch', 'sh', 'ss' and 'x', you add 'es'.
  *I bought two bru**shes** in bo**xes**, some mat**ches** and three wine gla**sses**.*

- When you form the plural of most nouns ending in 'f' or 'fe', the 'f' or 'fe' changes to 'ves'.
  *There is a knife on the shelf. There are two kni**ves** on the shel**ves**.*

- If a word ends in 'ff' just add 's'. *puff – puffs*

- When you form the plural of most nouns ending in 'y', two rules apply:

  – If a consonant comes before the 'y', it changes to 'ies'.
    *one lady – two lad**ies***

  – If a vowel comes before the 'y', just add 's'.
    *one monkey – two monk**eys***

Starter >

❶ Copy and complete the chart.
Write the plurals of the following nouns.

One	Two
cat	cats
brush	
banana	
bench	
scratch	
kiss	
thrush	
church	
brass	
fox	
lunch	
glass	

❷ Say which rule each plural applies to.

❸ Find five more words to illustrate each rule.

Practice ≫

4 Write the plurals of these nouns.
Look carefully at the letter before the final 'y'.

(a) berry (c) fairy (e) party (g) donkey
(b) valley (d) key (f) army

Write sentences using the words above as plurals.

5 Write the plurals of these nouns.
Check your answers in a dictionary. Some of these are tricky!

(a) hoof (c) cuff (e) staff (g) loaf (i) cliff
(b) scarf (d) thief (f) leaf (h) wolf

6 English contains a variety of irregular plurals.
Write the plurals of these words.

Singular	Plural	Singular	Plural
man		foot	
woman		tooth	
child		mouse	

Extension ≫≫

7 Some words have two forms of plural.
Look in a dictionary and find the plurals of these words.

automaton, criterion, larva, stimulus, appendix, formula, focus, stratum, synthesis, index

8 Some nouns are only used in the plural, e.g. 'scissors'.
Copy and complete these sentences with the correct form of the noun.

(a) Blue denim is made into thousands of pairs of _____ every year. I wear my _____ all the time.
(b) In Texas, most farmers earn their living by breeding _____ for meat.
(c) He spilt the drink all over his _____ so he looked odd just wearing his jacket.
(d) 'I just want to say _____ for everything you have done for me.'
(e) After the burglary we rang the _____ immediately and they arrived within five minutes.

Feedback ↩

Some of the words we use in English come from foreign languages and follow the rules of those languages for making plurals.

Objective ·····>

- To revise and extend work on verbs, focusing on verb forms.

Grammar Focus

- **Verbs** may be written in different ways, depending on the **job** they do. The chart below explains some verb uses.

Verb	Use	Examples
Interrogative	To ask questions	*Were you there?*
Imperative	To give orders, commands, requests	*Search for it!* *Please help me!*
Active	Where the subject of the verb performs the action	*Fred drove the car.*
Passive	Where the subject of the verb has something done to it	*The car was driven by Fred.*

Starter >

❶ Copy the sentences. Underline the interrogative verbs used in the questions. The first one is done for you.

- ⓐ *When are we going to the cinema?*
- ⓑ Will Jane come to school today?
- ⓒ Have you seen my pencil case?
- ⓓ What time does the film start?
- ⓔ Who has left the football team since last season?
- ⓕ Why do I have to do my homework on a Saturday?

❷ Write a question using each of these verbs:
  ⓐ are ⓑ have ⓒ come ⓓ gone.

❸ Decide which of the following are interrogative statements. Say why.

- ⓐ I wonder whether Fred will go to the match.
- ⓑ He asked me if I was going to the match.
- ⓒ Are you going to the match?

Practice ≫

4 Copy the instructions.
Underline the imperative verbs. The first one is done for you.

Programming a video recorder

<u>Switch</u> on the set. Press the timer button. Change the data in any sequence you choose. Set the date of the recording. Set the programme number. Start the start time. Set the stop time. Press the OK button. If you want to finish press the clear button. Watch the programme later.

5 Write step-by-step instructions for one of these simple activities.
Underline the imperative verbs you use.

 (a) making toast
 (b) loading a computer disk.

Extension ≫≫

6 Rewrite this extract.
Change the passive verbs to active verbs.
Do it like this: **The chef <u>shaped</u> the bread dough and <u>placed</u> it ...**

The bread dough <u>was shaped</u> by the chef and <u>was placed</u> into a lightly greased bread tin. It was then covered by a damp cloth and was left to rise in a warm place for 40 minutes until it was seen to double in size. Whilst the bread was rising, the oven was heated to a temperature of 230 degrees. Finally the bread was baked for 35 minutes until it sounded hollow when it was tapped.

7 Explain any differences that you notice between the two versions, when using active and passive forms of the verbs.

Feedback ↺

Verb forms are influenced by what you want to express.
– The imperative form is used to instruct.
– The interrogative form is used to ask direct questions.
– The active form is used to be direct + personal.
– The passive form is used when the writer is more distanced + impersonal e.g. reports.

Objective ·····>

- To revise earlier work on verbs and tenses.

Grammar Focus 📁

- A **verb** is a **doing word** or a **being word**.

  The cat <u>scratched</u> my hand. It <u>was</u> painful.

- The **tense** of a verb tells us whether something is happening in the **past**, the **present** or the **future**.

  Present: *Now I <u>see</u> my mother.*

  Past: *Yesterday I <u>saw</u> my mother.*

  Future: *Tomorrow I <u>will see</u> my mother.*

- Verb tenses enable you to communicate in the correct 'time' with your reader.

  – Different types of text tend to use different tenses.
  For example, when you tell a story you are generally talking about the past.

  – When you give information you are directly talking to your reader in the present.

  – If you were giving a weather forecast you would express your views in the future tense.

Starter >

❶ Copy the chart.
Decide whether the words in the verb box are past or present tense. Write them in the correct column to complete the chart.

Present	Past
Now I …	Yesterday I …

Verb box
get, stopped, do, jumped,
catch, got, tried, told, did,
stop, try, caught, tell, jump

Practice »

❷ Copy the sentences. Underline the verbs.
By the side of the sentences, write which tense or tenses they are in:
Pr (present); P (past); F (future).
The first one is done for you.

ⓐ I *believe* that smoking *is* bad for you. (Pr)
ⓑ My mum went to the shops and bought me some chocolate.
ⓒ It will rain in the north-west.
ⓓ The scene of this story is France and it is very exciting.
ⓔ Scientists say that people will walk on Mars within the next hundred years.
ⓕ He brought his dog along every time he came.
ⓖ Some old people dozed in their rocking chairs on the porch.
ⓗ When the weather improves they will work in the garden.
ⓘ Flowers with strong scents encourage bees to live in your garden.
ⓙ Farjad swam and swam but he did not reach the dog in time.

❸ Rewrite each sentence by changing the tense of the verbs.
For example: I *believed* that smoking *was* bad for you.

Extension »»

❹ Here are some awkward verbs.
Copy and complete the chart.
The first one is done for you.

Verb	Yesterday I …	I have …
To swim	swam	swum
To write		
To begin		
To buy		
To choose		
To come		
To drink		
To eat		
To fall		
To forget		

❺ Add five more irregular verbs to the chart.

Feedback ↻

Reread your writing and check that you have used verb tenses correctly and accurately. It is often better to use one tense throughout a piece of writing.

Objective ·····>

- To consider the impact of changing parts of speech on the meaning of sentences.

Grammar Focus

- **Parts of speech** (nouns, verbs, adjectives, adverbs, etc) are the building blocks of sentences.
  If we change them in some way, we change the meaning or sense of a sentence.

- The way a word is **suffixed** often tells us what part of speech it is – whether it is a noun, a verb or an adjective.

  The green toad hopped along.

  The verb is 'to hop'. The 'ed' suffix tells us that it is past tense.

- The same words can be used as different parts of speech.

  'Leaf' can be used as a noun:

  The trees come into leaf in the Spring.

  It can also be used as a verb:

  He leafed through the pages of the book.

Starter >

❶ Two common ways of changing the form or tense of a verb are by adding 'ing' or 'ed'.
Copy and complete the chart.
Check in a dictionary if you are unsure about the spelling.
The first one is done for you.

Root verb	Verb + 'ing'	Verb + 'ed'
laugh	laughing	laughed
wash		
dream		
rest		
smile		
cry		
hurry		
grab		
drum		
skate		

Practice >>

2 Copy each sentence below and underline the verb.
Then rewrite each sentence using the 'ing' and 'ed' form of the verb.
The first one is done for you.

(a) Julius Caesar <u>invades</u> Britain.
Julius Caesar was invading Britain.
Julius Caesar invaded Britain.

(b) Paul copies Emma's address.
(c) Mr Patel walks quickly.
(d) The army defends the camp.
(e) Ben and Miguel try hard to pass their exams.

(f) The alligator snaps its jaws.
(g) My mum snores loudly.
(h) All the children behave well.
(i) Mum shops at the supermarket.
(j) My favourite rock band tours all over Europe.

3 State which tense has been used in each sentence.
For example: *Julius Caesar invaded Britain.* *(past tense)*

Extension >>>

4 Copy each sentence.
Change the noun in brackets into an adjective.

(a) The bush was full of (poison) berries.
(b) Max made a (sense) suggestion for once.
(c) It rained all week so the holiday was a (misery) experience.
(d) The book was so (value) I was afraid to touch it.
(e) I apologised for making such a (fool) mistake.

5 Write a sentence for each of the following words using it as the part of speech indicated.

(a) giant (noun)
(b) giant (adjective)
(c) lie (verb)
(d) lie (noun)
(e) fall (noun)
(f) fall (verb)
(g) ring (noun)

(h) ring (verb)
(i) pine (noun)
(j) pine (verb)
(k) along (preposition)
(l) along (adverb)
(m) through (preposition)
(n) through (adverb)

Feedback ↩

If you know about the functions of nouns, verbs, adjectives, etc. you can understand how to achieve the effects you need.

Objective ·····>

- To investigate ways of connecting clauses.

Grammar Focus

- A **clause** is a **group of words**.
  It can be used either as a **whole** sentence or a **part** of a sentence. It does not necessarily make a sentence in its own right. It usually contains a **verb** and a **subject**.
  This is a **single-clause** sentence:

  Tracey went to the shops.

  'Tracey' is the subject and 'went' is the verb.

- We can make a **two-clause** sentence by joining two single-clause sentences together with a **connective** such as:

  and, but, so, unless, although, how, which, that.

  This is a two-clause sentence:

  Tracey went to the shops   so that she could buy a CD
  [clause 1]   [clause 2]

- Sentences can also start with connectives.

  Because Tracey wanted a CD, she went to the shops.

Starter >

1 Copy each pair of single-clause sentences. Join them with a suitable connective to make one longer sentence.
The first one is done for you.

(a) I will not talk to her. I do not like her.
  *I will not talk to her **because** I do not like her.*
(b) The giant looked big. He was friendly.
(c) My bag was small. It was very heavy.
(d) The dog ran away. The cat hissed at it.
(e) There was no moon. It was difficult to see.
(f) The TV was annoying. It was much too loud.
(g) She held the shell to her ear. She heard nothing.
(h) I am friends with the lions. I am a little scared of them.

Practice »

2 Write out the sentences.
Join them up using the relative pronouns from the box.
Remember to use <u>who</u> for people and <u>which</u> and <u>that</u> for things.

> **Relative pronouns**
> *who, which, that*

(a) The vet looked at the cat. It had a serious wound.
(b) Sophie has a new boyfriend. He is a singer in a rock band.
(c) Michael was sent to see the headteacher. She kept him in after school.
(d) I spoke to the punk. He had bright orange hair.
(e) Our teacher has an old car. It is always breaking down in the rain.
(f) The cyclist shouted at the lorry driver. He had caused her to swerve.
(g) The referee booked the player. He had injured the goalkeeper's leg.
(h) She suffered from short-sightedness. It could be cured by wearing glasses.
(i) He enjoys those TV programmes. They are about wildlife.

Extension »»

3 Join up these sets of three single-clause sentences.
Make them into one longer three-clause sentence.
Use commas and connectives. The first is done for you.

(a) Our teacher walked into the hall. She sat at the piano. She started to play it softly.
Our teacher walked into the hall, sat at the piano and started to play it softly.
(b) The leopard climbed down from the tree. It crept through the undergrowth. It chased after the antelope.
(c) The two boys stood in front of him. He tapped them on the shoulder. He could not see any of the match.
(d) I cannot lift the bag with my hand. It is painful. I injured it two weeks ago.
(e) The castle stood on the slope. It was being demolished by the council. It was in a dangerous state.
(f) The manager shouted at the girl. She was late for work again. This was the fifth time in a week.

Feedback ↺

A clause can be used as a whole sentence because it contains a main verb and has a subject. Extra clauses may be added to sentences to make them longer and more interesting. You can join two clauses together using 'joining words' such as connectives or conjunctions.

Grammar Focus

- A **simple sentence** contains just **one clause**.

  A simple sentence **makes sense on its own**:

  My nose is red.

- A **complex** sentence contains a **main clause** and at least **one** other, **less important clause**.

  The less important (**subordinate**) clause **does not make sense by itself**:

  My nose was red   because I had a bad cold.
  [main clause]   [subordinate clause]

- Simple sentences can only provide basic information. A subordinate clause adds extra detail and interest to a sentence and makes it into a complex sentence.

Starter >

❶ Copy the sentences. Underline the verbs.
Write by the side of them whether they are simple (S) or complex (C) sentences. Explain why.
The first one is done for you.

(a) My books <u>are</u> in the desk. (S)
This is a simple sentence because it contains only one clause.

(b) She took my books as soon as the teacher looked away.

(c) Water leaked out.

(d) Water dripped out where the drainpipe was leaking.

(e) Our snowman melted yesterday.

(f) All the snow melted because the air temperature rose in the country.

(g) I visited Paris.

(h) We visited France where I saw many fascinating castles.

(i) All the dogs in the kennels barked loudly.

Practice >>

2 Match the parts of the sentences in the chart and write the ten complex sentences.

(a) I shall not go to Turkey	where the water came in.
(b) He loves rock music	unless you tell me who broke the window.
(c) It will be a disaster	although I may visit Greece.
(d) We called off the football match	whether or not you go to the concert.
(e) His sister fainted	until he finds out who stole the bike.
(f) There is a stain on the ceiling	before I get very cross.
(g) Mark will not give in	because he plays guitar in a band.
(h) Stop all that noise	unless I can phone him first.
(i) You will go to your room	when she won the lottery.
(j) It does not matter to me	so we returned the tickets.

Extension >>>

3 Make these simple sentences into more interesting complex ones by adding a subordinate clause to each.
You will find examples of helpful connectives in the Practice section.

(a) Sophie did not understand _____.
(b) The rider fell off her pony _____.
(c) It will not be possible to travel _____.
(d) She had three stitches in her knee _____.
(e) The wall fell down _____.
(f) It is best to check the train timetable _____.
(g) He visited the ancient city _____.
(h) Margie caught measles _____.
(i) She stood on the chair _____.
(j) The bike will go off the road _____.

4 Underline the subordinate clauses you have added to the sentences above.

Feedback ↩

- You could use 'who' to join two clauses if you are talking about a person.
- You could use 'which' or 'that' to join two clauses if you are talking about a place or a thing.
- There are many connectives you could use to introduce subordinate clauses, such as 'after', 'although', 'when'.

Objective ·····>

- To investigate ways of extending sentences.

Grammar Focus

- You can make your writing more interesting by **extending your sentences**. There are many ways of doing this and this unit helps you investigate just a few.

- You can ask yourself questions about the facts of what you have written:

  When? Why? How? Where?

  The answers to these questions will be **phrases** or **adverbial clauses**.

  Phrases are small groups of words. They form part of a sentence but not a sentence by themselves, because most of them do not contain a verb:

  The man walked down the road.

  When?

  The man walked down the road <u>in the early hours of the morning</u>.

Starter >

❶ Extend these sentences by asking 'When?'
Underline the phrase or clause you have added.

  ⓐ I need to do my homework _____.
  ⓑ My sister travelled to Egypt _____.
  ⓒ The temperature never rises above freezing _____.
  ⓓ The firefighters had put out the fire _____.
  ⓔ He fell into the river _____.
  ⓕ She walked down the country lane _____.
  ⓖ England won five-nil _____.
  ⓗ Two fans travelled to see the rock band _____.

❷ Extend these sentences by asking 'Why?'
Underline the phrase or clause you have added.

  ⓐ The owls flew from the nest _____.
  ⓑ It rained heavily _____.
  ⓒ In Lapland they have six months of darkness _____.
  ⓓ My sister sat on the doorstep _____.
  ⓔ Suddenly the room lit up _____.
  ⓕ Max decided to dig a hole in the garden _____.
  ⓖ I saw the woman take the bag from the bin _____.
  ⓗ Our teacher told us to read the book _____.

Practice >>

3 Extend these sentences by asking 'How?' and 'Where?'
Underline the phrase or clause you are adding.

(a) Jan went on holiday _____.

(b) He ran out of the room _____.

(c) Germany won the football match _____.

(d) Glaciers are frequent in Norway _____.

(e) He shouted from the back of
the class _____.

(f) Two hundred British troops died
in battle _____.

(g) My bike fell over the bridge _____.

(h) Max sat on the sticky bun _____.

(i) It was fun helping my uncle _____.

(j) Charlie Chaplin slipped on the banana
skin _____.

(k) Two jets shot overhead _____.

(l) The new girl shouted at the
teacher _____.

4 Reverse some of the examples above, writing the phrase first. For example:
He ran out of class to chase the thief.
To chase the thief, he ran out of class.

5 Does the meaning of the sentence change when you reverse the order?

Extension >>>

6 One way of extending your sentences is to add more detail.
Consider this simple format:
The dog followed the man.

This is not a very interesting sentence. Write more about the dog and the man.

Add an adjective: The brown dog followed the man.

Add another adjective: The brown dog followed the tall man.

Use a different verb: The brown dog shuffled behind the tall man.

Add an adverb: The brown dog shuffled painfully behind the tall man.

Add facts: The brown dog from the rescue centre shuffled painfully behind the tall man.

Add another adjective: The brown dog from the rescue centre shuffled painfully behind
the tall, burly man.

After extending this sentence, how do you feel about the dog and the man?

7 Follow the above format to make these 'uninteresting' sentences more detailed.

(a) The man walked down the road.

(b) Two boys came to school.

(c) The girl listened to the music.

Feedback ↶

Adding phrases makes sentences more
interesting and meaningful. You can extend
sentences by asking yourself questions such
as: Where? What? Why? When? How?

Objective •••••>

- To explore the use of conditionals.

Spelling Focus

- A **conditional sentence** tells you that an action happens, or will or might happen, because it **depends on something or somebody else**. The following **modal auxiliary verbs** are often used in conditional sentences: 'should', 'would' and 'could'.

- A **conditional clause** is a type of subordinate clause usually starting with the conjunction 'if'. Other conjunctions introducing conditional clauses include: 'unless', 'as long as', 'so long as', 'provided that', 'providing'. Here are some examples of conditional sentences. The conditional subordinate clause is underlined.

If it rains, the cat stays indoors.

We would go to the cinema if Dad drove us there.

If we had left earlier, we would have arrived on time.

You would not be in trouble, if you had listened to my advice.

He could not do his homework unless the TV was turned off.

You can watch TV provided you do your homework first.

Starter >

❶ Copy the sentences.
Underline the verbs in the main clause.
The first one is done for you.

(a) *She will be going to the ball if the Fairy Godmother arrives.*
(b) If I don't work harder, I will have to leave school.
(c) If I had passed my driving test the first time, I would not be so desperate.
(d) Whether she found it or not, she would have to tell her father.
(e) If you like snorkelling, I can recommend the Red Sea.
(f) If you had got up earlier you would have seen the sunrise.
(g) Life might have been easier for him if he had had more help.
(h) No one would notice if you left the party early.

Practice >>

2 Copy and complete the chart.
Write four other conditional sentences in each box.

If ...	I will ...
If I pass the exam	*I will go to university.*
If ...	I would ...
If I passed the exam	*I would go to university.*
If ... had ...	I would have ...
If I had passed the exam	*I would have gone to university.*

Extension >>>

3 Write sentences to illustrate the following rules:

• If the verb in the conditional clause is in the present tense, the verb in the main clause often uses 'will' or 'shall':

If I discover the answer, I will tell you.

• If the verb in the conditional clause is in the past tense, the verb in the main clause often uses 'would' or 'should':

If I knew the answer, I would tell you.

• If the verb in the conditional clause is in the past perfect tense, the verb in the main clause often uses 'would have' or 'should have':

If I had known the answer, I would have told you.

Feedback ↩

A conditional sentence tells you that what happens in the main clause depends for its fulfilment on something else happening in the conditional clause. For example:.
I would go on a lovely holiday if I won the Lottery.

Grammar Focus

- Words are **ambiguous** when they can have more than one meaning. Often, ambiguous phrases are **funny**.

  I saw an elephant in my pyjamas.

  (Were you wearing your pyjamas when you saw the elephant? Was the elephant wearing your pyjamas when you saw it?)

- **Pronouns** are used to **avoid repetition**.
  Trying to avoid repeating nouns, can sometimes produce an ambiguous statement.

  If your kitten does not like fresh milk it should be boiled.

  The pronoun 'it' should refer to the milk: *it should be boiled*. However, it sounds as if the pronoun 'it' refers to the kitten and as though *the kitten should be boiled*.

- To **avoid ambiguity** you often have to **restructure the sentence**.

  Milk should be boiled if your kitten does not like it fresh.

Starter >

1 For each of the following words write two sentences to show that the word can have more than one meaning.
Use a dictionary to help. The first one is done for you.

(a) spring
We drank water from the spring.
See the cowboy spring to his horse.

(b) match
(c) well
(d) mine
(e) blind
(f) seal
(g) fine
(h) ruler
(i) strike
(j) pound

Practice >>

2 Explain what is ambiguous in each of the following sentences.

(a) I paint myself in my spare time.
(b) I shot an elephant in my dressing gown.
(c) I have a cure for spots which I have developed over years.
(d) Keep these tablets in a cabinet and if you have young children in the house, lock them away.
(e) The bird picked up the insect and after breaking its shell on a stone, ate it.
(f) The sergeant made the soldiers take off their back-packs and then he threw them all in the river.

3 Rewrite the sentences above so that they have one sensible meaning.

Extension >>>

4 Explain the two meanings that each of the following sentences could have.

(a) The jeweller took the chain from her neck and polished it.
(b) You will all go outside and collect the rubbish left from yesterday, including the teachers.
(c) Whenever my sisters make gingerbread-men for me at school, they look really happy.
(d) The surgeon told his patient that he would feel no pain.
(e) Max asked him where he had left his homework.
(f) I enjoy eating spaghetti more than my friends.
(g) Ray told Ben that he had won some money in the lottery.

5 Write each of the sentences again to make the meaning clear. You may need to restructure the sentence or to split each example into more than one sentence.

Feedback ↩

To avoid ambiguity:

- use pronouns clearly so that it obvious who or what is being referred to
- do not change from third to first person in the middle of a sentence
- keep an adverb next to or near the verb it modifies
- keep together the parts of a sentence that talk about the same thing.

Objective ·····>

- To review the agreement between subject and verb.

Grammar Focus

- The **verb** is probably the most important part of speech. 'Verb' comes from the Roman 'verbum' meaning 'the word'.

- In any sentence, the verb must **agree in number** with the **subject**.

  – If the subject is singular, the verb must be singular.

  He is watching the television. (correct)
  He are watching the television. (wrong)

  – If the subject is plural, the verb must be plural.

  They were watching the television. (correct)
  They was watching the television. (wrong)

Starter >

❶ Rewrite these sentences correctly.
Change the verb in each so that it agrees with the underlined subject.
The first one is done for you.

ⓐ The <u>girls</u> was swimming in the sea.
  The <u>girls</u> were swimming in the sea.
ⓑ <u>He</u> bring the book to school every day.
ⓒ <u>They</u> goes to the club every Saturday.
ⓓ <u>One</u> of the cats were hungry.
ⓔ <u>Sanjit</u> do his homework in his bedroom.
ⓕ Our <u>teacher</u> give us a spelling test each week.
ⓖ Her <u>sweets</u> was in the desk.
ⓗ <u>She</u> see the bus and run for it.
ⓘ Why is <u>you</u> looking so glum?
ⓙ <u>We</u> comes to school by bus.

Practice »

2 Match up Column A to Column B to make sentences.
You may need to change verbs in Column B to agree in number
with the subjects in Column A.
Write out each sentence.

Column A	Column B
(a) One boy from our class	was all sorry to see the teachers leave.
(b) Two girls	is roaming around the park as if they are free.
(c) Our gerbils	are coming to visit us in the crime campaign.
(d) The police	is getting bigger every day.
(e) Lisa's football team	have gone to the fair.
(f) Those lions	was winners in the competition.
(g) My classmates	are hoping to do well in the match.
(h) My mum and dad	was hoping for a win on the lottery.

3 Write some new sentences, beginning with the phrases in Column A.
Check that the nouns and verbs agree.

Extension »»

4 Say which verbs the statements are from.
For example, **done** is from the verb **to do**.
(a) He done   (c) They was   (e) I been
(b) I seen   (d) We has   (f) She were

5 Explain why the forms of the verbs above are incorrect.

6 Write sentences using the verbs above correctly.
Make sure they agree with the subject in each sentence.

Feedback ↻

It is important to understand and
recognise the need for subject-verb
agreement in sentences.
If the subject is singular, the singular form
of the verb should be used.
If the subject is plural, the plural form of
the verb should be used.

Objective ·····>

- To use punctuation marks accurately to clarify meaning.

Grammar Focus

- **Punctuation marks** help make your **meaning clear** in your writing.

- Punctuation marks can make a lot of difference to meaning. For example, if a prisoner was given this decision:

EXECUTE. NO RELEASE.

it might be very depressing.

If it was punctuated like this:

EXECUTE? NO. RELEASE!

it would mean something very different.

Starter >

1 Copy this passage.
Put in the missing full stops.

I bought a box of baking powder and a batch of biscuits I brought a big basket of biscuits back to the bakery and baked a batch of big biscuits then I took the big basket of biscuits and a basket of big biscuits and mixed the big biscuits with the basket of biscuits that was next to the big basket and put a bunch of biscuits from the basket into a box then I took the box of mixed biscuits and a biscuit mixer and biscuit basket and brought the basket of biscuits and the box of mixed biscuits and the biscuit mixer to the bakery and opened a tin of baked beans

Practice >>

❷ Rewrite these pieces of speech.
Put in the correct punctuation so that they make sense.

   (a) there is no need to shout I am not deaf the old man said
   (b) are you going home already Linda Susan asked
   (c) superb I cried so you like it then he said

❸ Copy this poem.
Make sense of it by adding commas and full stops only.
More than one version is possible.

   The pack of cards
   I saw a pack of cards gnawing a bone
   I saw a dog seated on Britain's throne
   I saw a queen shut up in a box
   I saw an orange driving a fat ox
   I saw a butcher not a fortnight old
   I saw a greatcoat all of solid gold
   I saw two buttons talking of their lives
   I saw two friends who told their wives

Extension >>>

❹ Explain the different meanings created by the punctuation in each of these examples.

   (a) The sphinx which is in Egypt is an ancient monument.
      The sphinx, which is in Egypt, is an ancient monument.
   (b) Boys who are dirty must wash.
      Boys, who are dirty, must wash.
   (c) 'Son, I said go home.'
      'Son,' I said, 'go home.'

❺ Punctuate this example in two ways so the meaning is completely different.

     I'll tell him you said hello Miss he said

Feedback ↪

Punctuation can change or affect the meaning of sentences. To check that your punctuation makes sense, ask someone else to read your work. It soon becomes evident whether the punctuation you have used is accurate or not.

Grammar Focus

- **Semicolons** are part full stop and part comma. A semicolon can be used in two ways.

  – It can **balance two parts of a sentence or two main clauses**.

  The guide opened the door; he showed us into the room.

  – It can **break up lists** containing more than one word, like a comma.

  Before the picnic we packed everything, including a box for the plates and cutlery; cartons of sandwiches; a bottle of soft drink; a table cloth and serviettes.

- A **colon** is used in two ways.

  – It may be used to **introduce a list**.

  You will need the following: scissors, paper and a pencil.

  – It is sometimes used to **introduce direct speech** (before someone speaks).

  The girl remembered the warning: 'Don't look back!'

Starter >

1 Copy the sentences. Put in the semicolons.

  (a) It was spring the daffodils had come overnight.
  (b) I stood quietly on the platform soon the train would arrive.
  (c) Judy had not done her homework she would be in trouble.
  (d) This is what I want: a loaf of bread made from wholemeal flour two sticky buns but only the round ones with cherries on top and a large portion of steamed pudding with custard.

2 Copy the sentences. Put in the colons.

  (a) You will need the following two eggs, one pound of flour and some milk.
  (b) There was only one judgement possible death.
  (c) Please note the rule no food allowed in the computer room.
  (d) The referee shouted 'Get off the pitch!'

Practice »

3 Add semicolons or colons to these sentences.
Write out the correct versions.

(a) It looked as if he had no other choice he would have to tell the truth.

(b) The large wall was covered with pictures the smaller wall had nothing on it.

(c) Suddenly Tricia screamed 'It's a dirty great rat!'

(d) Elizabeth slept soundly on the bench the train passed by.

(e) Take note of the school's new address 99 Arcade Street.

(f) Please don't forget to bring these for the ski trip your passport, a woolly hat and a pair of warm gloves.

(g) The woods were quiet only the birds sang in the trees.

(h) I'll search the bedrooms you search the play area.

(i) In the back room the cats were asleep in the kitchen the mice ate the cheese.

Extension »»

4 Rewrite these advertisements from the Internet.
They need semi-colons and colons.

(a) Super American car for sale. This car is a fantastic bargain it is only ten years old there is no rust to be seen on it last but not least it goes like a bomb! Email Ray on ray@raycars.com

(b) Wanted urgently someone to teach my son. I want the following qualifications an ability to put up with excessive noise all day someone who can understand how the mind of an eleven-year-old works a person who can translate my son's language. Anyone desperate enough should contact Sue@helpparents.com

(c) Wanted enthusiastic music expert to work in music shop in Soho. Must have own transport. Mail address soho@musictogo.co.uk

(d) Here we go all antique doll collectors Victorian porcelain doll for sale, made in 1878. The following still original glass eyes, hair, clothes. Email address Margie@margie'sdolls.co.uk

Feedback ↵

Colons and semicolons are fairly sophisticated punctuation marks. Using them correctly will help you vary sentences for the effect you want to achieve. They are important for the 'style' of your writing as well as to help with the meaning.

Objective ·····>

- To secure knowledge and understanding of more sophisticated punctuation marks.

Grammar Focus 📁

- A **dash** holds words apart.
  It makes a change of direction in the sense of a sentence.
  It is **stronger** than a **comma**, but **not as strong** as a **full stop**.

  There is only one meal worth eating – spaghetti!

- **Hyphens** may look the same but they are smaller.
  They are used to keep words together to make the meaning clear.

- You can create **compound words** using hyphens.
  For example, in this sentence below, 'rose-pink' is a **compound adjective** to describe the dress.

  My mother-in-law wore a rose-pink dress.

- **Brackets** can be used like dashes.
  They can separate off a part of a sentence or put in an extra example.

  He was awarded a prize in school (not before time).

Starter >

1 Copy these words.
Put in hyphens in the appropriate places.

- (a) two passers by
- (b) son in law
- (c) the sport of hang gliding
- (d) X ray eyes
- (e) cut throat competition
- (f) a successful lift off
- (g) mass produced goods
- (h) to cross examine

2 Copy the sentences. Put dashes in the appropriate places.

- (a) There is not a room left in the hotel let me repeat: No Room.
- (b) Mark's mum the famous actress, as I found out later was on TV.
- (c) She wants to buy him a new suit I can understand why.
- (d) There is only one instrument worth learning the guitar.

3 Copy the sentences. Put brackets in the appropriate places.

- (a) He swam across the river as the picture showed.
- (b) You must give me your homework on Wednesday. Any homework after that will not be marked.
- (c) Switch on the video recorder see Starting Instructions on page 5.

Practice >>

4 Copy these sentences. Put in the missing dashes.

(a) James used to dye his hair pink but now he has dyed it green.
(b) John Smith is a famous rock guitarist one of the best.
(c) Lady Burns has many trees in her garden willows, elms and oak trees.
(d) I want to leave at twelve so make sure you are ready.
(e) There is only one person who can do it me!
(f) The dog a hairy beast jumped up at me.
(g) Try to watch the programme if you have time it's wonderful.

5 Copy the sentences. Add dashes or brackets where they are needed.

(a) He drank his tea it was already cold and moved to his desk.
(b) At Cambridge University he gained a degree an upper second.
(c) Jake got to the skateboard competition in time the competition started late.
(d) The lead singer unlike the other members of the group was tidily dressed.
(e) Most of the pupils lost interest the pop group had left the school.
(f) The detective's disguise not really a very effective one was easy to see through.
(g) The films all five of them lasted only a day.

Extension >>>

6 Rewrite this passage inserting brackets and dashes where appropriate.

More and more people young and old are taking up sailing. Look at the latest figures page 20 of the magazine which prove this. Good sailing and of course safe sailing is the most important thing to learn. If you are unsure of this, look back at the news reports about sinking boats. A great deal of sport sailing, rugby, soccer is dangerous when not played well. The most important thing is to learn rules as it were to sail by. The law makes insurance necessary before you sail but often a fatal omission it does not cover all dangers.

7 Explain the difference in meaning between the following.
Explain what compound words the hyphens make in each case.

(a) a hot-water tap
   a hot water-tap
(b) twenty-year-old houses
   twenty year-old houses
(c) a grand-piano seller
   a grand piano-seller

> **Feedback** ↻
>
> Punctuation helps you to achieve the effect you want and to make your meaning clear. More sophisticated punctuation, such as brackets and dashes, allows writers to communicate finer shades of meaning.

Objectives ····>

- To use punctuation to clarify and emphasise meaning for a reader.
- To review how dialogue is set out and punctuated.

Grammar Focus

- Only the words actually spoken should go inside the speech marks:

  Max said, 'I am not going to wear that.'

- Begin the first word the person says inside speech marks with a capital letter, as it is really the beginning of a sentence:

  The teacher shouted, 'Stop running!'

- Always use a comma or a colon before opening speech marks:

  Max replied, 'Well, OK then.'

- Use a punctuation mark before the closing speech marks:

  'I'll be glad when this lesson's over,' Max sighed.

- When a quotation is interrupted in mid-sentence, you do not need a capital letter when you re-open the speech marks:

  'Well,' said Anna, 'what do you think?'

- Always start a new line whenever a different person speaks:

  'Where are you going with my CD?' Max asked.

  'It's not yours. I bought it,' I replied.

Starter >

1 Copy the sentences.
Write the direct speech in speech marks.

(a) Please don't play with that water-pistol in the front room, said Dad.

(b) Dad, it's only got a bit of water in, I explained.

(c) Dad sighed and said, You are the most awkward child I have ever met.

(d) You're always going on at me about what I bring into the house, I kept on.

(e) I'll stop your pocket money if you keep on like this, Dad threatened.

(f) I stood up. That's not fair. Just because I brought a toy into the house.

(g) It may be a toy but it will spoil the new carpet, he shouted.

(h) It won't spoil anything, I replied.

(i) Then explain to me why there's a puddle near your feet, he said.

Practice >>

❷ Punctuate these sentences correctly.

ⓐ Come along Max said the teacher you're holding up the entire class.
ⓑ There are several ways of making pancakes the chef said but I think this is the simplest.
ⓒ Take the first turning on the right she said but don't drive too fast down the lane.
ⓓ That car is great value the dealer stated so make sure you snap it up quickly.
ⓔ If you vote for me said the candidate I can assure you that this constituency will be well looked after.
ⓕ I've just seen a man the comedian whispered with a lemon in his ear.

❸ Copy this passage. Put in the appropriate speech marks. Start a new line for a new speaker.

I don't think we can afford to go on holiday this year, said Dad But I've told all my friends we're going to Barbados. You promised, replied Max. That's all very well, but with the new digital television and all the clothes you bought we just can't make ends meet,' he explained. I've got to have the latest trainers, Dad, or they'll laugh at me. What am I supposed to do? asked Max, sighing. Just then Jo rushed in saying, Dad I need money for the trip to America next year.

Extension >>>

❹ Add punctuation to these two extracts of dialogue from *Alice in Wonderland*.

ⓐ Let the jury consider their verdict the King said, for about the twentieth time that day. No, no! said the Queen Sentence first – verdict afterwards Stuff and nonsense! said Alice loudly The idea of having the sentence first! Hold your tongue! said the Queen turning purple I won't! said Alice Off with her head! the Queen shouted at the top of her voice. Nobody moved. Who cares for you? said Alice (she had grown to her full size by this time).

ⓑ The Hatter opened his eyes and said Why is a raven like a writing desk? Come, we shall have fun now! thought Alice I'm glad they've begun asking riddles – I believe I can guess that she added aloud Do you mean that you think you can find out the answer to it? said the March Hare Exactly so said Alice Then you should say what you mean the March Hare went on I do Alice hastily replied; at least – at least I mean what I say – that's the same thing, you know

Feedback ↩

Check your punctuation carefully:
• Are the actual words spoken in speech marks?
• Have you used a new line for each new speaker?
• Have you put punctuation inside the speech marks?

Objective ·····>

- To understand the difference between direct and reported speech.

Grammar Focus

- **Reported speech** (or **indirect** speech) is speech which reports the substance of what was said or written rather than the exact words used by the speaker.

  Notice the difference in the way these two sentences are written.

  Direct speech: *'I like sweets,' Anna said.*

  Reported speech: *Anna said that she liked sweets.*

- In reported speech you report what has been said but you don't quote it word for word.

- You do not use speech marks in reported speech.

- Often the person of the verb changes: in the example above it has changed from 'I' (**first person**) to 'she' (**third person**) and the **tense of the verb** has **changed** from **present** ('like') to **past** ('liked').

Starter >

❶ Decide which sentences use reported speech and which use direct speech.
Copy the sentences which use reported speech.

  ⓐ 'We'll never get away with it,' she said.
  ⓑ She told the thief that he would never get away with it.
  ⓒ The mayor said that he was pleased to be at the match.
  ⓓ 'I will not put up with such nonsense,' I shouted.
  ⓔ Miss Smith told the reporter that she was not responsible for what had happened.
  ⓕ 'I am sure that you will win,' he said.
  ⓖ She told her children to be careful because she knew there were dangers in the forest.

❷ Change the examples of direct speech above to reported speech using the Grammar Focus to help.

Practice >>

3 Match the reported speech with the direct speech which says the same thing.

Reported speech	Direct speech
(a) She asked him not to do that.	'I will go to the show,' she said.
(b) The mayor refused to agree to it.	'Be quiet!' the teacher shouted.
(c) She said that she would go to the show.	'Please don't do that,' she said.
(d) The teacher insisted that they be quiet.	'I've won! I've won,' she shouted.
(e) She told everyone that she had won.	'I will not agree to it,' said the mayor.

4 Change these sentences from direct to indirect speech.

(a) 'Why do you want it?' the teacher asked.
(b) 'I have mended the computer,' boasted Bev.
(c) 'My mum's got a spare key,' he told the policeman.
(d) 'I don't know how long I spend on the Internet every day,' Ranjit said.
(e) 'Which is the quickest way to the cinema?' the tourist asked.

REMEMBER

Reported speech does not use speech marks.

Extension >>>

5 You are a reporter at a public meeting about whether smoking should be banned in public places in your town.

(a) Write down ten statements you might have heard at the meeting in direct speech. For example, *'I think smoking is dangerous for my children,' said Dr Patel.*
(b) Use the chart below to change your ten sentences into reported speech. For example: *Dr Patel went on to say that he thought smoking was dangerous for his children. She also pointed out that ...*

He	added	that
She	went on to say	
Miss ...	also said	
Mr ...		
	pointed out	
	thought	
In	his, her, the Doctor's ...	view
		opinion

Feedback ↩

Direct speech is not always relevant or appropriate in some texts. Direct speech makes what people say come to life. Reported speech is used where the subject matter needs to be distanced from the person who said it. In reported speech the person and tense of the verb often change.

Objective ·····>

• To review how to integrate speech and quotation into writing.

Grammar Focus

• When you **quote** someone else's words in your writing you acknowledge this by putting them inside **quotation** (or **speech**) **marks**. We tend to use **double inverted** (or **raised**) **commas** in direct speech in schools, although single inverted commas are often used in books.

  Macbeth says, "Is this a dagger which I see before me…?"

  Macbeth says, 'Is this a dagger which I see before me…?'

• **Titles** of books, plays, poems, songs and films are placed in quotation marks (or **italics**). Usually we use **single** inverted (or raised) commas.

• Sometimes we have to use quotation marks **inside** speech marks. Here, use single inverted commas when the main speech is in double inverted commas.

  "Who can tell me," the teacher said, "which character said 'I came; I saw; I conquered'?"

• Notice the position of the question marks in the two examples above .

  – In the first one, the quote is itself a question, so the question mark goes inside the closing quotation mark.

  – In the second one, the question mark goes between the closing quotation mark and the closing speech mark.

Starter >

❶ Punctuate these titles and quotations correctly.
Don't forget to use capital letters where necessary.

ⓐ The sun is a newspaper.
ⓑ Dickens wrote a tale of two cities.
ⓒ Outside the exam room the sign said silence please.
ⓓ My favourite film is gladiator.
ⓔ Hamlet's most famous line is to be or not to be.
ⓕ Written on the door was do not enter.
ⓖ The school play this year is the importance of being earnest.
ⓗ We have to study a mouse and his child by Russell Hoban this year in English.
ⓘ The book opens with the words the tramp was big and squarely built.

Practice >>

❷ Punctuate this speech correctly. Put in capital letters where necessary.

ⓐ I felt really sad for the prisoner said the lawyer all he kept on saying was I want my freedom!

ⓑ Who has forgotten their copy of the lord of the flies asked the teacher

ⓒ Max shouted if I hear those words now is the winter of our discontent any more I'll scream

ⓓ We will be travelling on the flying scotsman to Glasgow the guide informed us exactly the same journey as John Buchan took in his novel the thirty-nine steps

ⓔ Let me have the video for just one evening begged Raj I haven't seen bladerunner in that new version and I love the film

ⓕ I'm confused I said is macbeth really the most important person in macbeth

Extension >>>

❸ Punctuate the following passage correctly.

Two professors were arguing about literature I think queen elizabeth wrote shakespeares plays said the first there is all the evidence of royalty in king lear and hamlet and plays such as twelfth night and the tempest show that the writer must have been aware of court life don't be ridiculous said the other you surely don't think that a queen of england wrote all those magnificent speeches such as if music be the food of love play on as well as the quality of mercy is not strained or even those wonderful words what light through yonder breaks The first replied who else could have known about the wars of the roses in richard the second or about the problems of love in romeo and juliet of course said the first there is a theory that elizabeth was a man and that would give a whole new meaning to the play much ado about nothing

REMEMBER

Speech marks are also sometimes called 'quotation marks' or 'inverted commas'.

Feedback

Punctuating titles and quotations correctly is important for conveying meaning. For example, how would you know whether Macbeth was the name of the Shakespearean character or the title of a play unless quotation marks were used?

You should use double inverted commas in your writing.

Make sure you punctuate quotations inside speech marks correctly to avoid confusion.

Objective ·····>

- To investigate ways of combining and linking sentences in a paragraph.

Grammar Focus

- Connectives are **words** and **phrases** which can **join together ideas.**

  Some of the most common are 'and', 'but', 'or', 'in other words', 'finally', 'nevertheless', 'just then'.

  She was tired from swimming, nevertheless she helped her mum in the shop.

- The writer's or speaker's choice of connectives can alert the reader to the introduction of new topics or ideas.

  yet, finally, and, aswell.

- Some connectives show contrast.
  but, although.

Starter >

1 Copy the sentences and underline the connectives.

(a) The cat sat down and stretched in the sun.
(b) There were birds in the tree but they were quiet.
(c) The birds all flew off, so the cat had no reason to be there.
(d) She felt angry and flung the toy mouse into the air.
(e) Tibbles walked away, firstly looking both ways for enemies.
(f) The garden was empty, but she was still on guard.
(g) Even though she was not really hungry, she took a few mouthfuls of food.
(h) I felt sorry for her but was glad the birds had escaped.

Practice ››

❷ See how you can easily change storylines.
For example:

Mary had a little lamb <u>until</u> the wolf finally gobbled it up.

Its fleece was white as snow <u>but</u> that was only because it never went out to play.

And everywhere that Mary went <u>although</u> she didn't go far!

The lamb was sure to go <u>so</u> it became a real nuisance!

Add a connective and another idea to the end of every line of these nursery rhymes.

Little Miss Muffet Sat on a tuffet, Eating her curds and whey; Down came a spider, And sat down beside her, And frightened Miss Muffet away!	Little Jack Horner, Sat in a corner, Eating his Christmas pie; He put in his thumb, And pulled out a plum, And said, 'What a good boy am I.'

Extension ›››

❸ Use the connectives from the box below to complete the chart. This will show the functions of various connectives.

> *next, just then, as you can see, nevertheless, and, in other words, suddenly, after that, finally, or, but, until, consequently, although*

Order	Time	Argument	Explanation
First	Then	Therefore	Because

❹ Use one word from each section of the chart in a sentence of your own.

Feedback ↩

You should consider how you can construct sentences in different ways to vary them.

The most common way of reconstructing sentences is to join them together using connectives.

Note that the connective you use will determine the way you complete your sentence.

Objective ·····>

- To revise work on shaping ideas in paragraphs through contracting sentences.

Grammar Focus

- We often shorten sentences to make notes.
- Sometimes we can use **abbreviations**:

  USA – United States of America

- Sometimes we can use fewer words:

  a place where fish are kept in a house – an aquarium

- Sometimes we can combine sentences into shorter ones:

  The car stopped working. It stopped because it ran out of petrol.
  The car stopped working because it ran out of petrol.

- It is important that the style in which you write is appropriate to the **purpose** of your writing and to your **audience**.

Starter >

❶ Copy the chart.
Match the abbreviations to their meanings.

Abbreviation	Meaning
p.t.o.	Anonymous
k.p.h.	Road
Rd.	Avenue
Anon.	Please turn over
Ave.	Kilometres per hour

❷ Write the abbreviation for each of the following.

British Broadcasting Corporation; Before Christ; Square; Royal Society for the Prevention of Cruelty to Animals; Post Office

Practice >>

❸ Give one word for each of the following places.

ⓐ where fish are kept in the house
ⓑ where ships are unloaded
ⓒ where race horses are kept
ⓓ where plays are performed

❹ Write the meaning of each of the following in one word.

ⓐ a device for putting out a fire
ⓑ to leave your country to live in another
ⓒ to rub out
ⓓ a building for the treatment of sick people

❺ Write one or two words which will summarise the following.

ⓐ radio, magazines, tv, film, newspapers
ⓑ pigs, cows, goats, horses, sheep, chickens
ⓒ curtains, blinds, armchairs, dining table, cushions
ⓓ teachers, accountants, lawyers, vicars
ⓔ plates, cups, saucers, mugs, bowls

REMEMBER

Using accepted abbreviations is a useful way of shortening your text.

Extension >>>

❻ Combine each of these pairs of sentences into one shorter sentence.

ⓐ The car stopped working. It stopped because it ran out of petrol.
ⓑ We shall visit the zoo. We shall visit it as soon as possible.
ⓒ The workers squeezed the grapes. They squeeze them to make wine.
ⓓ The water drains away. It drains through the hole in the bucket.
ⓔ The fisherman lifted the fish. It was lifted clear out of the water.
ⓕ The remark was typical. It was typical of my sister.
ⓖ My mother is in hospital. She is there to have an operation.
ⓗ Our house is made of wood. It is built like this because it is cheap.
ⓘ He jumped the barrier. This happened because the car drove towards him.
ⓙ My computer is in the shop. It is being repaired.

Feedback ↶

When you are asked to make notes:
• write using your own words
• select important information
• communicate clearly.

Objective ·····>

- To revise work on developing, linking and completing sentences in paragraphs.

Grammar Focus

- When you **edit** your work you may wish to improve it by **contracting** (making shorter) your sentences, or by **combining** them.

- We can shorten sentences by **leaving out** some words.

  If we remove the adjectives from *the huge, fierce monster came nearer* the sentence would shorten to *the monster came nearer*.

- We can sometimes shorten sentences by **combining two sentences into one**.

  The car stopped. It stopped because it ran out of petrol.

  The two sentences above can be shortened to:

  The car stopped because it ran out of petrol.

Starter >

1. Make these sentences shorter by taking out all the words – adjectives, adverbs and phrases – which describe the nouns or verbs.
   The first one is done for you.

   a. My *long-lost* uncle *from Italy* sat *down quietly* and ordered a *very expensive alcoholic* drink.

   b. Our small black cat quietly chased the grey mouse into its dark hole.

   c. The small, fair-haired girl loved, above anything else, diving dramatically into the blue waters of the pool.

   d. The brightly painted clown, dressed in the wildest colours imaginable, fell comically from the white horse into the sand of the arena.

   e. My favourite cousin, Sarah, read her new story book enthusiastically.

   f. The new hotel guest, the famous film star, quickly phoned the local police.

   g. Jim, my favourite singer from my favourite band, kindly signed my leather-covered, battered autograph book.

   h. The whole class – Year 6 – was provided with money to visit the historic and dramatic pyramids near Cairo in Egypt.

Practice »

❷ Decide on the most important facts in these sentences and write them out as briefly as possible. For example:

The group of students attempted to climb the mountain but they did not reach the summit of the mountain.
Students failed to reach top of mountain.

ⓐ Two men were injured yesterday when their car hit a petrol lorry on the M25 motorway.
ⓑ The staff meeting at the school started at three o'clock in the afternoon.
ⓒ The ancient Egyptians embalmed the bodies of the dead with exotic preserving oils and then wrapped them up carefully in bandages.
ⓓ The Oscar for the best actress in a supporting role in a film this year has been awarded to Sarah Biggs – a previously unknown girl.
ⓔ Our new car was of a very large size and was red in colour.
ⓕ They were considerably outnumbered by the pirates, yet they would not give up their struggle to defend their ship.

Extension »»

❸ Edit this passage.
Write the four things that Pat had to do in the fewest words possible.

Pat was really busy. First she had to collect her baby sister from nursery and then she had to call in at the supermarket to buy a bottle of milk for their breakfast. She hoped they would have plenty of milk left. In her pocket was the electricity bill she needed to pay as well and … oh, she had to clean the car before she was allowed to have her tea.

REMEMBER

If you shorten sentences you sometimes have to change words and use connectives.

❹ Edit this passage.
List the four things that are responsible for the change in our weather.

There is no real agreement about why our weather has been so strange recently. Some scientists believe that the earth's axis is changing very slightly over the years. Others deny this and instead blame the greenhouse effect which is melting the polar ice-caps, causing the seas to rise and the land to get colder. The ozone layer is disappearing and to make it worse man is changing the course of many rivers and damaging the environment for all of us.

Feedback ↻

We can often improve our sentences by combining or restructuring them. When you are asked to make notes, it is important to select relevant information and communicate it clearly and briefly. Using accepted abbreviations is often useful when making notes.

Grammar Focus 📁

- A **paragraph** is a **group of sentences** about **one particular subject**.

- Paragraphs should contain **one clearly stated idea**, called the **topic** sentence.
  This is the key to understanding what the paragraph is about.

- The topic sentence will make a **general statement** and the **rest** of the paragraph will **illustrate** this.

- The sentences in a particular paragraph need to be **organised carefully** to make maximum sense.

- When the **subject changes**, **begin** a **new paragraph**.

Starter >

❶ Decide which of the following sentences could start a paragraph (be a topic sentence). Give your reasons. Consider the definition in the Grammar Focus before starting.

- ⓐ She could see that it would only cause trouble.
- ⓑ Slowly the sun rose and he breathed a sigh of relief.
- ⓒ Finally he could stand it no more and walked out.
- ⓓ Gilly saw the racing car and fell in love with it on the spot.
- ⓔ It was as if the scene was being played in slow motion.
- ⓕ Maxine knew it was not going to be her day when the bus was late.
- ⓖ He summoned up his courage and at last knocked on the door ready to apologise.
- ⓗ They wouldn't come now.
- ⓘ Then, just as he turned the corner he saw the car in the distance.
- ⓙ 'Today marks the anniversary of the school's foundation in 1823,' said the Mayor.

❷ Write a paragraph to complete any three of the topic sentences you have found.

Practice >>

3 Organise the paragraphs below in a sensible order. Write the sequence of letters. Explain why you chose that particular order.

A. Surprisingly, although the Internet is having a huge effect on our lives, there is no English word for the @ symbol. In German it is a 'klammeraffe' meaning 'little monkey' and in Danish it is a 'snabel' meaning an elephant's trunk. It says something that the most popular symbol in English does not even have a name!

C. The Internet is one of the most important communication media of our lives today. Endless amounts of data are transported around the world in seconds at the flick of a switch – and millions of people are affected by this revolution.

E. Since then, entire languages have been developed for this global communication medium – like 'emoticons' where symbols reflect the emotions of the writer ('-)' means 'tongue in cheek') – and in 1988 the first virus for the Internet was invented by an American student.

B. This was followed by the development of the @ sign to become an essential component of e-mail addresses and in 1973 the first international connection between University College London and the Royal Radar Establishment in Norway was made.

D. Ray Tomlinson could not guess at the impact of his first message in 1971 – 'QWERTYUIOP' – when researchers in Utah and California set up the first long-distance links between computers. Ray combined two computer programs already in existence – and history was made.

F. Over 10 billion e-mails are dispatched every day and a conservative estimate predicts that this will rise to 35 billion in just three years. These figures show how millions of us are now involved in this technological phenomenon.

Extension >>>

4 Use the following sequence of events to structure and write a newspaper article entitled:

A Global warming – winters becoming shorter
- A doubling of carbon dioxide concentrations would increase av. temp. by up to 4 degrees.
- By 2050 scientists predict sea levels up to 2 feet higher – impact.
- UK climate warmer now than since 17th century.
- 1990s warmest years on record. Winters 40 days shorter.
- UK – 1% of world population – produces 2.3% of world's carbon dioxide.
- Activities, e.g. burning coal and gas to generate electricity, to blame for carbon dioxide levels.
- Climate change – caused by increased levels of carbon dioxide and other polluting greenhouse gases in earth's atmosphere.

For each of your paragraphs you should:

- choose your topic sentence

- add appropriate detail

- organise your sentences appropriately.

Feedback ↻

Here are some points to help you remember when to begin a new paragraph:

- a change of time
- a change of place
- a change of speaker
- a change of topic
- each paragraph should be about a new idea and should have a topic, or main, sentence.

Objective ·····⟩

- To review ways of opening, developing, linking and completing paragraphs.

Grammar Focus

- **Paragraphs** need to group ideas in a sensible order. This is important so that your reader can follow logically what you are trying to say.

- Many paragraphs contain ideas that are presented in **chronological** (time) order. This is essential for texts such as recipes, instructions and stories.

- The words that you use to link ideas in a paragraph are important.

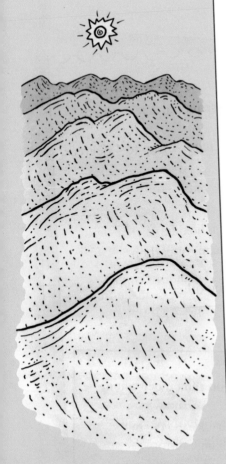

Starter ⟩

❶ Identify the topic sentence in each of these paragraphs. Explain why you have chosen it.

A. Oxfam is the abbreviation made from 'The Oxford Committee for Famine Relief', which was founded in 1942. It was set up in Oxford to help the victims of war, persecution and disaster. Today its focus has changed but it still faces huge problems worldwide. It is not simply a money-giving organisation, although it does send huge amounts of supplies to disaster areas. It teaches people to feed themselves and to grow food. It pays for medical help to prevent disease and improve people's lives. When you make a donation to Oxfam you know you are making a difference to someone's life somewhere in the world.

B. It is a simple procedure to grow crystals yourself. You need a jam jar and access to your kitchen. Boil some sugar in a pan, slowly adding it to water until no more will dissolve. Leave it to cool. When the solution has cooled, pour it into the jam jar. Take a sugar cube and suspend it in the solution on a piece of cotton. Use a pencil across the tip of the jar to help tie and suspend the cube. In just a few days the crystals will start to grow.

❷ List each of the points made to illustrate the main theme of the two paragraphs.

Practice »

❸ Arrange the events below into the correct order and write the sentences in a series of short paragraphs. There may be more than one possible order.

(a) He walked further towards this.

(b) Carefully he placed the worm over his hook, making sure it was fixed.

(c) Fred instinctively gripped the rod as it came alive.

(d) He felt the moment where the line would snap if the strain increased so he let it go a little more.

(e) He could see the dark water in the centre of the river where the trout would be.

(f) Then he pulled a few metres of line from the reel and threw the line and hook out into the centre of the river.

(g) It floated downstream with the current and he held firmly onto his rod, balancing the handle in his hand.

(h) Suddenly there was a tug.

(i) It bent double and the line was speeding away from him.

(j) He knew what he must do – but could he really do this.

(k) 'This is no trout,' he thought. 'This is a pike.'

(l) He was breathing heavily in excitement. He had never caught such a large fish before.

(m) Before he could think again the fish shot out of the water, twisted and dragged more line.

(n) Fred held tight and then was aware of the slackness. The fish had got away.

Extension »»

❹ Read the notes. Use them as the basis for writing three paragraphs. Think carefully about how you will start your sentences and how you will organise them.

Vandalism – young people today – boredom – no sense of community – overcrowded homes – high-rise flats – truancy – no value in education – work needed – heavier fines.	Deserts – definition less than 10mm rain per year – without rain, no plants will grow – ground bare – no roots – swept away – no food for people. But some deserts do have rain – all at once – cause flash floods – .	Metals – two classes – pure metals – made of elements and alloys – iron and copper – bronze is an alloy – made by mixing molten copper and tin – brass – made from copper and zinc.

❺ Write another paragraph to add to each of the subjects above.

Feedback ↻

When planning your paragraphs, think of the main idea you want to communicate. This should be your topic sentence. List under this all the things you want to say about it. How you group these sentences together will influence the way someone reads your paragraph.

Objective ·····>

- To investigate the vocabulary, organisation and conventions of ICT texts.

Grammar Focus

- Every subject area has a **specialist vocabulary** – words and expressions used in that subject. This ensures that ideas in the subject can be clearly and precisely explained.

- Different subject areas also have different **language conventions** – they expect certain **writing styles** and certain uses of grammar.

- In **Information and Communication Technology (ICT)**, many words are new because the subject is so new. Many traditional words are used in a different way. ICT allows people to communicate quickly and informally, and the written style of e-mails and faxes, for example, reflects this.

Starter >

❶ Sort the vocabulary from the box into the correct columns of the chart.
Explain your choice.
Use a dictionary to find the meanings of any difficult words.

> alphabet, binary, glossary, byte, cable, CD-ROM, angle, cursor, database, delete, disk, kilometre, electronic, hardware, icon, isosceles, input, interactive, interface, metaphor, Internet, keyboard, megabyte, memory, modem, harmony, monitor, multimedia, mouse, tempo, network, password, processor, program, baptism, scanner, server, software, spreadsheet, stereotype, virus

ICT vocabulary	Vocabulary relevant to other subjects
binary	alphabet

❷ Add five more words or expressions that are specific to ICT.

Practice ≫

3 Read the passage.

> From: ray@macronet.net
> To: steven@grammarnet.gov
> CC: Headteacher, Events Manager
> Subject: Invitation to speak
> Date: 3 June
>
> Dear Professor Richards
> Thank you for agreeing to speak @ the opening of the Education Exhibition on 2 Jan 2002.
>
> You will be expected to speak at 9.30 am for 20 mins on a subject of your choice, and then take questions form the audience for a further 10 mins.
>
> Please forward me a brief biography for the programme and any AV requirements for the day. Please attach any files and send them to events@macronet.net
>
> I will be in touch closer to the day. I look forward to meeting you. Please contact me if you need any further information.
>
> With all good wishes,
> Ray Smudge
> Chief Events Coordinator

Find examples of the features of e-mail from the above and write a summary of them.

Hints:
Subject, Address, Details for easy reply, Greeting, Introduction, The main part of the communication, Conclusion, The ending, Uses first person, Use of abbreviations/symbols

Extension ≫≫

5 Rewrite this e-mail appropriately so that it sounds more formal.

> From: ray@macronet.net
> To: steven@grammarnet.gov
> CC: Headteacher, Events Manager
> Subject: Important person talking (too much!)
> Date: 3 June
>
> Hi there Max, How are you doing there? I'm in desperate straits! I need a big speaker for our new education event – Education Exhibition 2002. The big government type I had has cried off. You know all these important people and I thought you would able to use your expertise (flattery again) to find me someone. We can give them promotion and lots of press coverage and will even pay for a hotel the night before! No expense spared. Help me out here mate – send anything to events@macronet.net
> Cheers now. :) Ray

Feedback ↺

The subjects you learn in school use different vocabulary and language conventions. For example, how you write about a science experiment will be different from how you write about a country you are studying in Geography or how you communicate using e-mail. This is because the audience and the purpose of your writing are different in each case.

Objective ·····>

- To analyse the vocabulary and stylistic conventions of the main text-types.

Grammar Focus

- Every subject area has a **specialist vocabulary** – words and expressions used in that subject. This ensures that ideas in the subject can be clearly and precisely explained.

- Different subject areas also have different **language conventions** – they expect certain **writing styles** and certain uses of grammar.

- In **History** you will often be asked to write something to **persuade**. These pieces develop ideas with supporting facts to present a logical argument.

- Often, these words help with argument:

   thus, therefore, consequently, as a result, in view of this, this suggests that, but, alternatively, it could be argued that, nevertheless, on the other hand, it has been suggested

Starter >

1 Sort the vocabulary from the box into the correct columns of the chart. Explain your choice.
Use a dictionary to find the meanings of any difficult words.

> bias, castle, cathedral, dramatise, Catholic, chronological, citizen, improvise, colonisation, constitution, document, dynasty, playwright, government, spotlight, imperialism, independence, sketch, parliament, Protestant, reign, perspective, republic, revolution, spectrum, siege, trade, traitor, director

History vocabulary	Vocabulary relevant to other subjects
bias	

2 Add five more words or expressions you would expect to write in History.

Practice >>

3 Read the passage. Find examples of the features of persuasive writing in it.

Slavery in the Ancient World

Slavery is awful in any society and the societies of Ancient Greece and Rome are often criticised for the treatment of slaves. However, we cannot criticise people because what we believe today is different from them. We must judge the ancients on their own terms.

The idea that all men are born equal was unthinkable in the ancient world. Historical evidence shows us that Athens in the 5th century BC was the cradle of democracy and all citizens – rich and poor – had a say in government. But not slaves. For example, a slave in Ancient Rome could be tortured to test evidence in court.

The ancients believed that work was something not done out of choice but out of necessity. Philosophers such as Aristotle believed that civilised life was for leisure and men should enjoy nobler pursuits in life.

In conclusion, although slavery is considered to be an awful institution today, the ancients cannot be blamed for using slaves in their civilisations as attitudes and beliefs were very different then. Historians have shown that the life of a slave was not always one of unmitigated misery.

Hints:
Use of connectives to direct the argument and to link paragraphs, e.g. 'furthermore'. Use of general terms for people involved, e.g. Europeans. Use of present tense (but use of past tense where historical evidence is given). Use of technical vocabulary, Starts with a statement of the position of the writer. Arguments backed up with evidence. Paragraphs have topic sentences at the beginning. Conclusion offered in the form of a summary. Use of impersonal language – no use of first or second person pronouns.

Extension >>>

4 Choose a topic from history that is the subject of some debate.
Write a piece to argue your ideas.
Use the following format and use what you have learned so far in this unit.

TITLE:

Your main idea – your 'thesis'.

What position do you start from in the argument?

Your arguments:

Argument 1:

Details to prove this:

Argument 2:

Details to prove this:

Argument 3:

Details to prove this:

Your conclusion (a summary):

Feedback ↻

The subjects you learn use different vocabulary and language conventions. You will learn how to adapt your writing style to suit the different subjects. For example, how you write an essay in History will be different from how you write about a particular country you are studying in Geography.

Objective ·····>

- To analyse the vocabulary and stylistic conventions of the main text-types.

Grammar Focus

- Every subject area has a **specialist vocabulary** – words and expressions used in that subject. This ensures that ideas in the subject can be clearly and precisely explained.

- Different subject areas also have different **language conventions** – they expect certain **writing styles** and certain uses of grammar.

- **Recounts** retell or recount past experiences. In fictional writing these are often based on personal experiences. Non-fiction recounts tell us about lives or journeys, for example biographies or autobiographies.

Starter >

❶ Sort the vocabulary from the box into the correct columns of the chart.
Explain your choice.
Use a dictionary to find the meanings of any difficult words.

alliteration, apostrophe, latitude, autobiography, desert, atmosphere, clause, dialogue, figurative, longitude, genre, grammar, imagery, erosion, metaphor, settlement, myth, narrative, narrator, onomatopoeia, estuary, paragraph, personification, preposition, urban, rhyme, scene, simile, soliloquy, vocabulary

English vocabulary	Vocabulary relevant to other subjects
alliteration	

❷ Add five more words or expressions that are specific to English.

Practice >>

❸ Read the passage from an autobiography of a Victorian woman traveller.
Find examples of the features of a recount in it.

A pretty mare, hobbled, was feeding; a collie dog barked at us, and among the scrub, not far from the track was a rude, black, log cabin, as rough as it could be to be a shelter at all, with smoke coming out of the roof and the window. We diverged towards it; it mattered not that it was the home, or rather den, of a notorious 'ruffian' and 'desperado'.

I called the hut 'a den' – it looked like the den of a wild beast. The big dog lay outside it in a threatening attitude and growled. The mud roof was covered with lynx, beaver and other furs laid out to dry, and antlers of deer and old horseshoes lay about the den.

Roused by the growling of his dog, the owner came out, a broad, thickset man, of middle height, with an old cap on his head, and wearing a grey hunting suit much worse for wear (almost falling to pieces, in fact), a digger's scarf knotted around his waist, a knife in his belt and a revolver sticking out of the breast pocket of his coat.

Hints:
Details: who, what, when, how? Key events in chronological order. Talk about specific people involved. Usually written in the past tense – except diaries. Paragraphs indicate changes in time or theme. Include only important information

Extension >>>

❹ Write your own recount about 'A Visit to …'.
This could be either fictional or factual.
Use the format below and the techniques discussed in this unit.

TITLE:
Who?
What?
When?
How?

Feedback ↻

Every subject in school uses different vocabulary and language conventions For example, how you write a personal experience in a recount will be different from how you write about a country you are studying in Geography.

Objective ·····>

- To revise the conventions of standard English.

Grammar Focus 📂

- Five hundred years ago, when English started to be written down, rules were made and **standard English** was said to be the correct version of **written** English. It is the kind of written English used in most books.

- **Non-standard English** is often used in **everyday speech**. We often say things differently from the way in which we would write them.

  - **Standard English:** *We haven't any money.*
  - **Non-standard English:** *We ain't got no money.*

Starter >

1 Choose the correct form of the verb in brackets and write out each of the sentences correctly.

(a) There (was/were) two clocks on the station wall.

(b) 'Look. Here (are/is) the newspaper you lost yesterday,' I replied.

(c) My grandma (give/gave) me a new computer for Christmas.

(d) All my toys (has/have) my name written on them in case they are stolen.

(e) Each actor (was/were) given an extra bow at the end of the show.

(f) Tracy (did/done) her homework before school.

(g) No, Mike (aren't/isn't) allowed to go to the cinema this evening.

(h) (Do/does) anybody want to go to the pantomime this year?

(i) My mum (don't/doesn't) allow us to go to concerts by ourselves.

Practice >>

2 Rewrite the sentences below in standard English.

(a) The two boys was fighting in the street.
(b) Each of the sweets in the packet were wrapped in coloured foil.
(c) 'I ain't done nothing,' my brother shouted.
(d) We done the washing up after dinner.
(e) My mum said she didn't want nothing for her birthday.
(f) The policewoman give me a warning when she caught me in the orchard.
(g) Them two girls wasn't allowed out to play.
(h) I never saw nobody at the concert because the seats were at the side.
(i) Louis hadn't been nowhere near the window when it smashed.

Extension >>>

3 Rewrite the conversation below in standard English.

'Who's got me sweets? I ain't got none left. I spent a quid on them yesterday. I bet that Ray is stuffing his face with them.'

'There isn't no point in blaming me. The sweets was in my locker. Me and John was going to eat them tomorrow. I bet that bloke over there has got them.'

'No. He don't know nothing. I already asked him. He give his sweets away to someone else. Those kids isn't coming today. That means we haven't got no food today.'

'Wait a mo. Look in that cupboard what's to your left. I think that's the food what I bought the other day. Do anyone know if it belongs to anyone? I don't want no trouble if we eat it.'

'No problem. All the adults has gone to work. Great ... this food is wicked.'

Feedback ↩

In writing we usually need to use standard English. We should not use:

• Double negatives: *I **never** went **nowhere**.*

• Adjectives as adverbs: *We painted the picture **lovely**.*

• Singulars and plurals mixed up in subject-verb agreement: ***We was** running very fast.*

Objective ·····>

- To revise formal styles of writing.

Grammar Focus

- **Formal styles of writing** are used for 'formal' situations. You find formal styles of writing:
  - on official forms
  - on signs in official buildings
  - in important rules and regulations.

- Some people say that using such language makes understanding easier.

- Some people say it is old-fashioned and makes understanding much more difficult.

- There is a difference between speaking and writing. Speech is linked to people, their body language, facial expressions and what you know of them. Non-standard English is often used in speaking.

- Writing is more impersonal and clues to meaning have to be supplied by the writer. Standard English is more often used in writing.

Starter >

1 Read the box below.

> Dear Sir or Madam, Yours faithfully, Dear Mum, Cheers Jim, I hope this finds you in the best of health, How are you?, Best wishes, Yours sincerely, I refer to your letter of last month, Love and kisses

Copy and complete the chart.
Put the phrases and sentences from formal and informal letters into the appropriate columns.

Formal style of letter	Informal style of letter

2 Which type of letter is written in a more friendly way? Why do you think this is?

Practice >>

❸ Copy these sentences from the emergency procedure leaflet on an aeroplane.

ⓐ For your safety you must comply with all the signs.
ⓑ Emergency exit: cabin door operation.
ⓒ Seats 6A and 6B are designated as emergency seats only.
ⓓ If you meet these criteria, please identify the exit nearest to you.
ⓔ Review the information on the back of this card.
ⓕ Keep your belt fastened unless crew assistance is required.
ⓖ Infant flotation devices are available.
ⓗ Identify yourself to a crew member to be re-seated.
ⓘ To sit in the exit seat you must be independent of responsibilities for another person.

Underline the words which are examples of formal writing.

❹ Rewrite the examples using simpler, less formal words.

❺ Which set of instructions do you think are the best to have on a plane? Why?

Extension >>>

❻ Rewrite this application form in less formal language.
Complete the form for an adult.

Applicant's surname _____
Full forenames _____
Maiden name _____
Marital status _____
Name of spouse _____
Distinguishing marks _____
Country of residence _____
Nationality _____
Previous occupation and employer _____
Dependants _____
Contact number _____
Signature _____
The countersignatory should also endorse the reverse side of one photograph.
You may redeem the voucher according to the instructions on the reverse.
Return this at your earliest convenience.

Feedback ↩

The use of English depends upon purpose. A formal letter needs a different style and uses different conventions than an informal letter.

Objective ·····>

- To investigate past and current language trends.

Grammar Focus

- Our language is continually changing. English did not start to develop into its modern form until about 1500. Ever since then, it has been constantly changing, absorbing words and grammar from other countries and languages.

- We can still understand English written hundreds of years ago even though the grammar of the language is often different: they used different acceptable forms of sentence construction and punctuation.

- New words and constructions are constantly entering our language, especially as technology changes the way we communicate.

- It is interesting to see where words come from. For example, *cigarette, anorak, bungalow* come from different cultures and have been with us since the nineteenth century.

Starter >

❶ Use a dictionary (an etymological dictionary would be most useful) to find which languages the words below originated from.

- (a) anorak
- (b) ballet
- (c) hamburger
- (d) restaurant
- (e) bamboo
- (f) kiosk
- (g) guerrilla
- (h) robot
- (i) pyjamas
- (j) umbrella
- (k) bungalow
- (l) tomato
- (m) sugar
- (n) lager
- (o) thug
- (p) yoghurt

Practice >>

❷ Read this passage written in 1600 about Ben Jonson's reaction to the new discovery – tobacco.

(Printers used the letter 'f' to represent 's' at this time – but not always!)

> By godf me: I marvel what pleafure or felicitie they have in taking this rogish Tabacco; its good for nothing but to choke a man, and fill him full of fmoake and emberf; there were four died out of one houfe last weeke with taking it, and two more the bell went for yester-night, one of them (they say) will ne'er efcape it, he voyded a bushell of foote yesterday, upward and downwards. I'ld have it prefent death, man or woman, that should but dele with a tabacco pipe; why it will ftifle them all in the end as many as ufe it; its little better than ratf bane.

Write a version of the passage in modern English. Look up any difficult words in a dictionary.

❸ Make a list of all the grammatical and language features that vary in the two versions. For example, Jonson uses semicolons where we would be more likely to use full stops.

Extension >>>

❹ Write the current meanings of the words below relevant to the internet. If they have been used in different contexts before, write what other meaning they have too.

(a) cookie
(b) chunky
(c) floppy
(d) Trojan horse

(e) smileys
(f) spam
(g) bookmark
(h) history

❺ Find out what Shakespeare meant by these words and explain what we understand by them today.

Shakespeare's word	What it meant then	What it means now
naughty	Worth nothing – an insult	
wicked		
nice		
vulgar		
humour		

Feedback ↺

We have taken words and grammar from many different countries. Many words are no longer in general use. Think about the new computer words you use and how many will remain in use. The original meanings of many words have changed or have had a new meaning added, e.g. 'cool', 'wicked'.

Objective ·····>

* To explore differing attitudes to language.

Grammar Focus 📁

* **Slang**: Groups of people who speak the same language often invent words to make their language special and private. For example, Cockneys in London often talk in slang.

  I'm wearing my whistle and flute. (suit)

* **Accent**: People speak the same language but it sounds different because of the way they say it.

  'Toity poiple boids' could be someone from New York saying *'Thirty purple birds'*.

* **Dialect**: People may speak the same language but they have different words for things and ways of saying them. For example, a Jamaican writer might say:

  'Him head eena de air' for *'he kept his head in the air'*.

* Speaking or writing in slang, accent or dialect is not necessarily incorrect. It all depends upon the audience and the purpose of your writing. To ensure that most people understand what you are trying to communicate it is better to use **standard English**.

Starter >

❶ Read these examples of Cockney rhyming slang.
Copy and complete the chart.
Match the beginning to the rhyme.

Slang phrase	Rhyme
whistle and flute	the wife
apples and pears	feet
trouble and strife	my head
Barnet fair	your mouth
plates of meat	a suit
loaf of bread	my hair
north and south	money
bees and honey	the stairs

Practice »

2 Copy and complete the chart.
What words do we use in English for these American words and phrases?
Use a dictionary to help you.

American word or expression	Word or expression we would use
clothes pins	clothes pegs
an elevator	
vest	
sidewalk	
ice-box	
chips	
an apartment	
checkers	
subway	

3 Add four more examples to the chart.

Extension »»

4 Afferbeck Lauder in his book *Let's Talk Strine* wrote down how he thought Australians talked.
Read these examples to yourself and write out what you think the writer wanted you to understand. For example, ***scettin lairder*** = it's getting louder!

ⓐ 'It gives me grape leisure …'
ⓑ 'Thenk smite.'
ⓒ 'Dimension.'
ⓓ I got asplit nair dyke.
ⓔ Fitwer smee ide go.
ⓕ 'I gunga din, the door slokt.'

5 He also wrote a book called *Fraffly – the language 'spoken in the West End of London'*.
For example: ***fraffly caned a few*** means ***frightfully kind of you.***
Read the following and work out the names of the places in London.

ⓐ Wessmin Streppy ⓑ Mob Lodge ⓒ Girlda Skrin ⓓ Connor Bess Street ⓔ Rich in Spock

6 Read the following and work out the men's names.

ⓐ Author ⓒ Darkless ⓔ Deffid
ⓑ Goddon ⓓ Grairgrair ⓕ Grem

7 Write examples in a similar way of another kind of speech or dialect known to you.

Feedback ↻

There is a difference between speaking and writing. Speech is linked to people, their body language, facial expressions and what you know of them. Writing is more impersonal and clues to meaning have to be supplied by the writer.

Published by Letts Educational
The Chiswick Centre
414 Chiswick High Road
London W4 5TF
Tel: 020 89963333
Fax: 020 87428390
email: mail@lettsed.co.uk
website: www.letts-education.com

Letts Educational Limited is a division of Granada Learning Limited, part of the Granada Media Group.
© Ray Barker and Louis Fidge 2002
First published 2002

ISBN 1 84085 669 6

British Library Cataloguing in Publication Data
A catalogue record for this book is available from the British Library.

Acknowledgements
The publishers would like to thank the following for permission to use copyright material. Every effort has been made to trace copyright holders and to obtain their permission for the use of copyright material. The author and publishers will gladly receive information enabling them to rectify any error or omission in subsequent editions.
Illustrations: Topham Picturepoint pages 52, 56, 58 and 60 and Harry Bell page 62

Commissioned by Helen Clark
Project management by Vicky Butt and Aetos Ltd
Editing by Diana Roberts and Jane Otto
Cover design by Bigtop Design
Internal design by Aetos Ltd
Illustrations by Sylvie Poggio Artists Agency: Nick Duffy, Tony Forbes and Roger Langridge
Production by PDQ
Printed in the UK by Ashford Colour Press